Going on Holiday!

Maureen Lewis

holidays to suit you

jmc
summer
sun
march to october 2002

JMC Holidays Limited a member
of the Thomas Cook Group

Thomas
Cook

Heathrow **express**

PRENS
REVISTE

EUROPEAN UNION

UNITED KINGDOM OF
GREAT BRITAIN
AND NORTHERN IRELAND

EXP CARNET
02
HEATHROW EXP
HEX ONLY
Conditions of carriage available on r

every 15 minut

Kodak
ULTRA
SPORT

waterproof

Thomas
Cook
T

LOS JAZMINES

HOTEL   HOTEL

Contents

holidays to suit you

jmc

summer sun

march to october 2002

JMC Holidays Limited a member of the Thomas Cook Group

Thomas Cook

HOLIDAY essentials

Costa del Sol

This one?

FROM £319

HOLIDAY essentials UK EXCLUSIVE see page 13

☀ ☀ SUPERIOR

Hotel Los Jazmines
Torremolinos

Los Jazmines offers comfortable accommodation. Although the complex is at the quieter end of Torremolinos there is still plenty going on making it an ideal holiday base.

Location
- Playamar beach is only 50m away

Facilities
- Swimming pool set in grass sun terrace
- Buffet restaurant by the pool
- Nearby mini-market
- Lounge with bar and satellite TV

For Children
- Section of pool; cots free

Rooms have 2 or 3 beds, satellite TV and full bathroom. Some rooms have a balcony with sea view and some are bungalow style. Prices are based on 2 adults sharing a room on **Bed and Breakfast.**

Child prices: age limit 12.

95 rooms.

Official rating: 2 stars.

Booking the holiday

Booking Form   Sunny Days Holidays

Name (Mr, Mrs, Ms) First name [_____]   Surname [_____]

Address: [_____]

Street [_____]

Town [_____]   Post code [_____]

Phone number [_____]   Email [_____]

Number of people in the group:

Adults [_____]   Children [_____]

Number of rooms needed: [_____]

To (resort name) [_____]

Hotel [_____]

From (date) [_____]   To (date) [_____]

Flight from [_____]   airport to [_____]   airport

Flight departure time [_____]

Flight return time [_____]

Special requests (e.g. sea view)

[_____]

25%   Doc: 22.3M/7.2M

7

Packing for the holiday

Clothes
shorts
t-shirts
sandals
swimming things
jumper
underwear
pyjamas
sunhat

Toiletries
suncream
soap
toothpaste
toothbrush

Other
camera
film
sunglasses

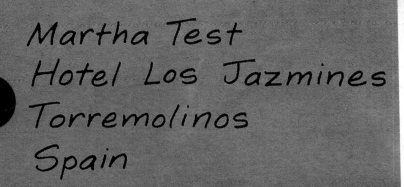

Martha Test
Hotel Los Jazmines
Torremolinos
Spain

Travelling to the airport

TARIFF INC. VAT.

UP	TO	30	Mins	£ 1.80
''	''	1	Hr	£ 3.30
''	''	1½	Hrs	£ 4.70
''	''	2	''	£ 5.90
''	''	3	''	£ 8.50
''	''	4	''	£11.00
''	''	5	''	£13.50
''	''	6	''	£16.50
''	''	9	''	£24.00
''	''	12	''	£31.00
''	''	24	''	£36.00

LOST TICKETS will be **CHARGED** at **FULL DAILY RATE**

MAJOR CREDIT CARDS ACCEPTED

Boarding the plane

Landing in Spain

Abflug
Departures
Salidas
T2

Toiletten
Toilets
Aseos

Llegadas
BUS

Salidas

Rent a car
Terminal de carga

Tiendas del Aeropuerto

MULTITIENDA

CHOCOLATE
SOUVENIRS
TOYS
LEATHER GOODS

PRENSA
REVISTAS

CHEMIST · APOTHEKE · PHARMACIE

Arriving at the hotel